MW01173417

Crochet for Absolute Beginners

Step-by-Step Guide to Learn Crocheting in No Time.
Easy Instructions with Pictures and Illustrations.

By

SARAH TUNISIAN

Sarah
Tunisian

GET YOUR BONUS NOW!

Thank you for purchasing Crochet for Absolute Beginners!
I'm excited to offer you a FREE download of my Crochet Journal To help you
keep track of your crochet projects.

Crochet Journal

It's a tool I designed to help you record all the details
of your projects, including a picture of the completed
crafts and a sample of the yarn you used.

To download your **FREE** copy, **scan the code below**
and follow the instructions. Happy crocheting!

TO DOWNLOAD YOUR BONUS SCAN THE CODE BELOW

This bonus is 100% FREE, no strings attached

TABLE OF CONTENTS

Introduction

Crochet is a centuries-old skill named after the French term crochet, which means "hook." Crochet is a peaceful and enjoyable activity that is simple to pick up. The most common crochet aim is self-evident: Crochet lovers want to finish crochet projects, which are usually useful, beautiful, or helpful in some way. Afghans, baby booties, baby blankets, scarves, caps, granny squares, handbags, shawls, tote bags, and other crafts are popular. You can crochet to make various items, including socks, jewelry, and curtains.

It is also feasible to crochet a variety of components for use in other projects. Crochet trimmings and edgings, for example, are popular crafts that may be used on knitted, crocheted, and sewn items. You might, for example, purchase some towels, socks, and pillows and crochet an edge on each.

One of the most extraordinary things about crochet is that you do not need to know much to create beautiful things, yet there is always something new to learn. With only a little knowledge of materials and the fundamental single crochet stitch, you will be able to create scarves and blankets in no time. You will become creative with the things you make as you learn more about materials, various stitches, methods, and reading patterns. This book will teach you the fundamentals of crochet, as well as a few popular stitches.

Crocheting is a delicate craft that can create lovely presents for others and things for your home and wardrobe. Begin by learning a few fundamental stitches, then progress to more complex basic stitches. First, choose the size and type of most comfortable hook for you. Then start with basic yarns and simple designs, and you will be an expert in no time.

Chapter 1: Choosing the Perfect Crocheting Supplies

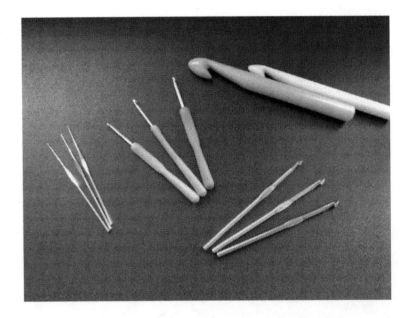

Crochet is one of the favorite crafts of many people since it doesn't need a lot of supplies to get started. You will just need yarn and a crochet hook. (Suggestion: you can crochet with your fingers and other fibers than yarn, but it is better to start with the fundamentals.)

1.1 Choosing The Yarn

Which kind of yarn should you purchase? If you already have yarn at home that you wish to work with, it is quite acceptable to do so. However, certain yarns are simpler to learn to crochet with. If you are heading to the shop to buy yarn, here are some things to keep an eye out for:

- A light shade of a solid color. Yarn that varies color throughout (commonly referred to as variegated yarn) and yarn that is dark in color will make learning more complicated since it is more difficult to tell where your stitches should go.

On the left, smooth yarn, on the right, textured yarn

- When you look at the yarn, it seems to be extremely smooth. Many kinds of fibers are available these days, and novelty yarns with bumps and other textures. These are all excellent crochet, but you will want to go with yarn with a simple texture while learning the art. This yarn is available in various fibers, but cotton, wool, and acrylic are the most popular. People may learn on any of these materials, so discover what works best for you. Cotton is an excellent starting place since it has the greatest stitch definition. (The term "stitch definition" simply refers to the ability to see each shape of your crochet stitches.) It is simpler to learn about things when you can see them clearly.) Another excellent option is a very smooth acrylic that is also extremely cheap.

- Yarn with a weight of the medium. You may find extremely thin yarn (and even thread) and very thick yarn in crochet; each yarn weight has a distinct impact and function. The best choice is to use a medium, average-weight yarn when first learning.

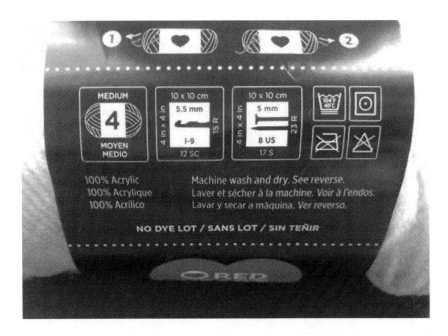

Spend some time learning to read a yarn label if you haven't already. This label contains a wealth of information, and since they are generally consistent, knowing about one will educate you about most of the yarn you may wish to buy. First, check for the number on the yarn that indicates the weight; for example, a worsted weight yarn is size 4. That is plainly stated in the box on the left side of the yarn label shown above.

1.2 Choosing The Crochet Hook

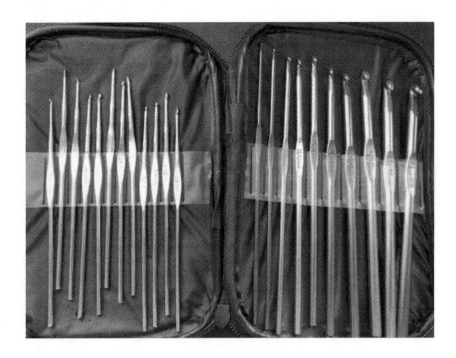

It is OK to attempt learning with what you have if you already have a crochet hook in your collection and do not want to invest in new materials. Most of the time, the yarn you have will work with the hook you have. But if you have to purchase a new hook anyway or have trouble learning to crochet with the one you have, there are a few things to keep in mind when buying your first crochet hook.

- Choose a hook size that complements your yarn. This information may be found on the yarn label in certain instances. You may also look this up on the internet. Although you are free to use any yarn with any hook size, the results will be drastically different, and using hooks designed for yarn other than what you are using will be more challenging as a novice. Consider using a size H crochet hook if you have chosen a medium worsted weight yarn. Tip: The yarn label will usually indicate which hook is suitable for that yarn. Next to the number 4 that indicates yarn weight, it recommends a size I crochet hook on the yarn label shown above. Hook sizes in the United States are represented by letters like these and millimeter values that correlate to those letters.

- Choose a hook size that is convenient to work with. Hopefully, the suggested hook size for your yarn will feel appropriate, but if it doesn't, you may move up or down a size. For example, you could have selected a size H crochet hook to go with your outdone weight yarn, but you might use a size G or size I crochet hook instead.

- Important note about sizing: Thread crochet is done with tiny crochet hooks. Because the size of these hooks differs from that of regular yarn crochet hooks, obtain additional information before using them.

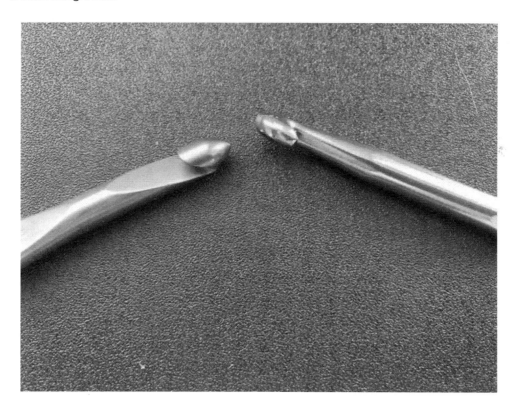

- Heads of crochet hooks A crochet hook may have two distinct "heads": inline and tapered. You may find it helpful to study more about each kind later on, but for now, just remember that the inline is pointier, flatter, and deeper than the tapered form. The tapered is on the right, while the inline is left in the image above. Both can work for you, so all you need to know for now is that if you are having difficulty learning to crochet, it may be worth it to switch to a different hook than the one you have been using.

- Handles made from crochet hooks. Hook handles come in a wide range of materials, shapes, and sizes (plastic and aluminum are common, but glass, wood, acrylic, and bamboo are other options). Most crochet hooks include a thumb grip, making crocheting easier compared with those that do not. There are also ergonomic handles available for crocheters who suffer from hand discomfort.

- Overall, the best advice is, to begin with, the basics. Choose aluminum or plastic mid-size crochet hook with thumb rest, and make a note of the kind of hook head it has if you need to try another later.

How to Hold Your Crochet Hook?

The essential thing to remember about holding the crochet hook is that you will have to experiment to find the position that feels the most natural to you. Another important point to remember is that individuals hold their hooks in two main ways: "like a knife" and "like a pencil." You will hold the hook similarly to how most people hold those two tools, as their names indicate. Let's look at it more closely:

- **Knife Hold for the Crochet Hook**

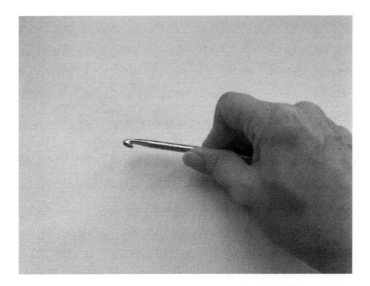

Start with one of them and see if you can develop a version that works for you. If you still can't get the hang of it, try the other approach with your modifications. Tip: Take a pencil out of a desk and a knife out of a drawer and hold them both in your hands to observe how you usually handle these tools. Use this method to practice holding your hook. Also, keep in mind that what seems uncomfortable at first will most likely become second nature very soon.

- **Pencil Hold for the Crochet Hook**

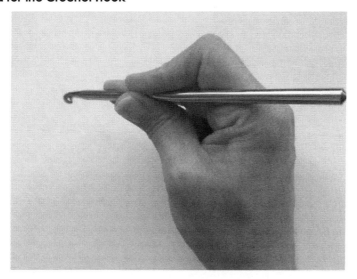

The hook is held between the second finger and thumb in the pencil grip. Your third finger may provide extra support or curl into your fist, preventing you from grasping the hook.

1.3 Crochet Threads

Crochet thread is available in a variety of sizes, kinds, colors, and amounts. Threads are scaled according to their weight, represented by a number; the lower the number, the thicker the thread. Size 3 thread, for example, is considerably heavier than size 8. Sizes 3, 5, 8, 10, 20, 30, 40, and above are available. Sizes 30 and 40, which are excellent for lacy designs, are less often employed. The meterage (yardage) of crochet thread balls varies, as stated on the package. The number of balls and thread size needed to finish a job are typically specified in the instructions.

1.4 Dye Lot

Manufacturers add a dye lot number on each label because the color of crochet threads may change significantly from dye lot to dye lot. This number ensures that crochet thread from the same dye lot number has the same color. It is suggested that you purchase all of the crochet thread for a project simultaneously and with the same dye-lot number.

Chapter 2: Understanding Crochet

Most of you would have come across crochet in one form or another, whether as clothing or accessories. Like a loop and bright thread colors, the structure is intriguing to spice up the monotony of living things and daily fashion. It is the technique of producing fabric by interlocking loops of thread, yarn, or strands of other materials with a hook, rather than the name of the fabric itself. This name derives from the French and means small hook.

2.1 The History and Evolution of Crochet

You can use a crochet hook to create a crochet from wood, metal, or plastic materials. It may be produced either commercially or in artisan workshops. Crochet thread is composed of mercerized cotton with a smaller diameter and a denser pile than regular yarn.

In 1823, the term crochet was first used in the Dutch journal Penelope. The earliest English mention of clothes made of fabric created by looping yarn with a hook is in Elizabeth Grant's Memoirs of a Highland Lady. There is evidence that French tambour needlework and crochet have a link despite their English roots. Diderot's Encyclopedia, published in 1763, detailed the old manner of manufacturing. Bone, ivory, or wooden hooks and steel needles have been described in many different texts.

Crochet was first used in Ireland during the Great Irish Hunger (1845–1849) in the 19th century as famine relief. Crocheted lace was a source of income for impoverished Irish artisans. Crocheting was also taught in schools as part of the famine relief effort. The Irish migration brought the craft to the Americas.

Irish crochet is said to have been invented by Mademoiselle Riego de la Blanchardiere. In 1846, she released the first book of patterns. Irish lace gained popularity in Europe and America, and it was mass-produced until World War I.

2.2 The crafting surge

From the late 1940s through the early 1960s, there was a resurgence of interest in home crafts, especially in the United States, with many innovative crochet patterns for potholders, colorful doilies, and other household goods released. The new generation became interested in crocheting and utilizing bright colors in the late 1960s and early 1970s.

Crochet styles changed towards the conclusion of the Victorian period. Crocheted lace's texture and stitching grew ever more complex. The preference for white or light-colored threads has grown. Crochet designs were hard to get by after World War I. The majority were reduced copies of designs from the early twentieth century.

Crocheting and other handcrafts regained popularity in the early twenty-first century, thanks to new designs and vivid colors. Materials may be purchased online or at craft stores. It is possible to self-teach the skill by reading about it.

Crochet is making a comeback in the fashion world. One of the most fundamental crochet patterns is heavily used in Christopher Kane's Fall 2011 Ready-to-Wear collection. Furthermore, it is a skill that designers have shown on the famous reality program Project Runway on many occasions. Individual hobbyists may now sell and share their patterns or creations over the internet.

2.3 How is crochet made?

It's all about the way you make it. The 'starting chain' is crucial in the creation of crocheted cloth. The number of stitches necessary for the number of chains required to reach the proper height of the first stitch in the first row and the first row of fabric defines the length of the beginning chain.

Each stitch may have more than two chains. Each row of crochet is made up of one or more major chains. The hook is then raised to the row's first stitch height. The stitch height determines the number of chains required for turning.

2.4 How to use crochet

You can use it to depict shapes in hyperbolic space, which are difficult to duplicate in other media shapes. It's also useful for shapes that are tough to comprehend when seen in two dimensions.

After discovering that paper models were fragile and difficult to construct, mathematician Daina Taimina developed this technique in 1997 to create robust, lasting models of hyperbolic space. These models let you bend, twist, and otherwise manipulate space to understand better concepts like how a line in hyperbolic space may seem curved but is straight. Iris Van Herpen, a Dutch fashion designer, has used it extensively in her different designs.

2.5 Crochet for charity

It was customary for individuals to make clothes and other items and then give them to troops during the war. Crocheting clothes and donating them to patients, hospitals, and newborn infants is still a common tradition today. Occasionally, people may band together and produce something for a particular charitable cause. Making hats and donating them to cancer treatment centers for people receiving chemotherapy is becoming more popular. Pink hats and scarves are popular throughout October. After that, the profits will be donated to breast cancer charities. Crochet for Cancer, Knots of Love, and Soldiers' Angels are a few organizations devoted to utilizing their art to benefit others.

2.6 Advantages and Surprising Benefits of Crochet

- Easier to retrieve from mistakes because of fewer live stitches

- Easy to learn

- Cost-effective in investing in the required materials

- Cheap way of making accessories and clothing

- Portable

- Several benefits in terms of health, for example, toning of eyes and muscles in the fingers, stress relief, staves off Alzheimer's

2.7 Can You print crochet fabric?

You can now, without a doubt! If you're crocheting your material, the kind of yarn you choose will determine whether or not you may color it. On the other hand, Crocheted apparel does not need expert crocheting skills.

Now that you know what it is you can use fabric swatch bundle to be creative, including a Crochet Lace Fabric that you can print on.

2.8 The 9 Most Important Things to Know About Crocheting

As a beginner to crochet, it is ok to get eager to get started and create amazing things. There are so many beautiful designs and techniques to master, and you can't wait to make that adorable item all by yourself, can you? Awesome. So, without attempting to scare you, there are a few things you should be aware of before you begin.

These are some things that will come in useful when you start working on that adorable design. So let's get started.

1. Be aware of the words you are using.

Did you know that the same kind of crochet stitch has multiple names? There are various variations of the same language for crochet, just as there are distinct shapes of American English and British English (and Aussie English). The tricky part is that both 'languages' employ the same terms, but their meanings are different. In a British design, a double crochet stitch (dc) would be called double crochet, the same stitch as a British treble crochet stitch (tr) in American terminology. In contrast, it is called single crochet (sc) in an American pattern. Isn't it puzzling?

No matter the method you choose, it is important to double-check the terminology for each design before beginning. It is simple to locate a conversion chart online if you find a design that uses the opposite crochet vocabulary to the one you have learned.

The same is true for wool weight and hook sizes, and it is referred to differently in different countries around the globe. Some modern hooks marketed in Australia now have both the U.S. size name and the millimeter measurement, making it simpler to identify the size you need regardless of whatever language your pattern is written in; nevertheless, if your hook has the 'wrong' size name, there are lots of conversion tables available.

2. In the Round vs. Rows

Flat items are typically crocheted row by row, which involves working in a straight line until you reach the end, then flipping the object around and working in the other way. You are effectively sewing in a zigzag pattern. But, still in the same direction since you rotated the work.

Crocheting in the round implies stitching in the same direction as a spiral without rotating the work at the end of a row, resulting in a tube. This doesn't mean you have to stick to cylinder shapes; you can make virtually any shape by adjusting the number of stitches at different places.

Except for accessories like coats, most toys and dolls are made round using a basic single crochet stitch (U.K. double crochet) to keep the gaps small and the filling in place. Because larger stitches create greater gaps, smaller stitches are often utilized for stuffed toys, and larger stitches are typically used for larger items (making it easier and quicker to complete). Your item will be more flexible if you use a bigger stitch.

3. Where should you place your hook?

The hook always passes under both the front and back loops of the stitch to draw a new loop through unless the design says otherwise.

Have you ever noticed how each stitch or chain shapes a V? The front loop is the side of the V nearest to you. The back loop is the side of the V that is farthest away from you.

The top of the stitch is the space between these two loops - the gap where you put your hook. The post is the knotted portion on each side of this area that you can see from the side in a completed item.

When you put your hook into the top of the stitch, two bits of wool should appear on top of the hook - these are the back and front loops of the stitch into which you are putting a new stitch. When you yarn over, you should have three lines of wool on your hook, and when you pull that yarn through, you should only have one line of wool on the hook. I hope that was clear.

A pattern may instruct you to crochet just through the front loop or only through the rear loop, but always put the hook under BOTH loops unless otherwise stated.

4. Keep it loose

One of the most common beginner's mistakes is pulling the wool too tightly. It is easy to get into this poor habit when you are first learning how to handle the hook, the wool, and the work in progress simultaneously, mainly if you are concerned about the wool sliding off the hook! Pulling the wool too tight, on the other hand, makes things more difficult.

The stitches have to be loose enough to comfortably enter the hook and then pull through, with enough give to allow the work to expand slightly without losing its form. Keeping your fingers flexible can help keep them from cramping up too much.

5. Make use of a stitch marker.

To correctly follow an amigurumi pattern, you must first understand where each round begins and finishes. You can keep a record of it by counting stitches as you go, but using a stitch marker is considerably simpler – and takes up less mental space, allowing you to crochet on any vehicle while doing other things like conversing or watching your favorite Netflix program.

You may purchase specific markers for this purpose or simply use a safety pin. Instead of using a pin, you can also use a piece of leftover wool in a different color if you work on repeated small rounds, like a doll's leg, so that you do not have to stop every ten stitches from changing the pin. Others have suggested using a bobby pin, so use anything you have on hand that won't harm your yarn or get in the way as you stitch - whatever works for you!

Another suggestion is to be consistent with your stitch marker placement - determine whether you will put your stitch marker in the final stitch of each round or the first stitch of your next round and do it the same way every time. It is the simplest to put the marker in the final stitch of the previous round after you have finished the first stitch of the new round since this keeps the hook out of the way. It means you will have to remove the marker to finish the round, but you have to be aware that the stitch with the safety pin is always the final stitch for that round.

6. Concentrate on one stitch at a time.

It is tempting to get right in without learning all the required stitches when you come across a really attractive design. And it may be OK if you are a fast learner with a good memory who can learn on the go without becoming confused. But, for the most part, taking the degree of difficulty into account is very beneficial, even if it requires a little patience.

Begin by learning and mastering the fundamental stitches of single crochet (sc), slip stitch (ss), and double crochet (dc) before progressing to more complicated stitches such as treble, half double, and so on. Amigurumi is simple to create since it mainly consists of single crochet stitches. If you are going to make amigurumi, try understanding the invisible decrease (inv dec) quickly since you will need it for any spherical shapes like doll heads and so on.

Make a sample with only that kind of stitch to familiarize yourself with the abbreviations and each stage of a new stitch. Performing the same stitch again and over until you are completely secure in it will cement the technique into your brain and give you a decent sense of what the result will look like in terms of the pattern it produces, the size, etc., and so on. It is also useful to have a paper copy of the stitch instructions nearby to refer to them quickly.

7. Sewing skills are very useful.

Many crochet objects are made up of separate pieces that are then stitched together.

8. Do not be worried if you make a mistake.

Your first year of crocheting will perhaps be littered with blunders. But, guess what? That is OK. It is all part of the learning and improvement process. Plus, crochet errors are simple to correct: unravel to the point where things begin to go wrong and re-do from there. (If you haven't pulled too tight – see tip #4 – this will be a LOT simpler.)

Untangling many rows of work may sound tedious, but it is simpler than unpicking a complete seam in sewing or attempting to retouch a messed-up painting.

Re-doing a part may seem to be a lot of effort, but it is well worth it if the result is something you are pleased with. It is easy to say, "Oh well, it is only a minor blunder, but it is done," and leave things alone. But if you do not like how it appears, you will be unhappy that you didn't attempt to change it. Sure, unraveling and starting again takes time, but it is well worth it when you can look at the final product and be completely satisfied with what you have created.

9. Be kind to yourself.

It takes some time and practice to learn a new talent. Expecting to be excellent at anything right away is unreasonable.

When you try anything new, you will get very thrilled when your initial tries come out better than anticipated, only to be disappointed when the second, third, and fourth attempts fail. It is tempting to give up at this point and say, "Perhaps this isn't my thing after all," but if you stick with it and do not expect to be producing masterpieces right away, you will get there.

Chapter 3: Terms and Vocabulary

Beginning mesh- Making a chain of five stitches and then skipping the next two stitches creates a starting mesh space or beginning space. In the next stitch, double crochet, then double crochet again.

Back loops (bl)- These are the loops on the top of a stitch farthest away from you in a crochet stitch. A back loop single crochet stitch is identical to a standard single crochet stitch, but instead of using both loops as in the preceding stitch, it utilizes the back loop. Crocheting back loops gives your stitches a distinct feel and adds a ridge to your work.

Crochet applied slip stitch- This stitch is a finishing method for adding a basic, elastic border to your project's edges. Pull the hook through the cloth, bringing up a loop of yarn through the edge, with the right side of the product facing you. Then, put the hook a little distance away with the yarn over the hook. On the hook, pull up another loop of yarn. Continue to work your way around the perimeter of your project.

Afghan stitch- The afghan stitch, also known as the simple Tunisian stitch, is a basic crochet pattern that resembles small squares with a vertical bar. The afghan stitch necessitates using an afghan hook, which has a cap at the end to keep stitches in place.

Back cross-stitch (bcr)- This stitch is a crochet stitch that may be used to create eyelets. Skip the next stitch and decrease in the next stitch as you crochet. Put the hook from back to front in the skipped stitch and double crochet.

Basic mesh- To produce an open weave cloth, a basic mesh is crocheted by skipping stitches. Garments, housewares, accessories, and embellishments may benefit from basic mesh.

Back post (bpsc)- The rear post single crochet stitch (bpsc) is a variant of the basic single crochet stitch. Crocheting the back post gives your cloth a ribbed appearance. Crochet a yarn around the post underneath the stitch you are working on, and then perform single crochet as usual to create a back post stitch.

A starting block (bb)- This is an increase made by crocheting two double crochet stitches for the top of an increasing block.

Berry stitch (berry st)- This is a method for making baubles that look like tiny berries in your crocheted item. Chain three stitches, then put the hook into the next stitch, yarn over, and pull through the thread to create a berry stitch before proceeding with your design; yarn over and draw the yarn between two loops on the hook.

Blanket stitch- The blanket stitch is made up of two single crochet stitches and one double crochet stitch. Blanket stitch is a fundamental crocheting technique that may be used to make crocheted blankets or afghans. Butterfly loom is a hand-held instrument for weaving open mesh yarn squares that may be crocheted or slip stitched together to make scarves, blankets, rugs, and other items. The butterfly loom is a hinged board in the center and has notches on either side for hooking thread during the weaving process.

Chain stitch- This is the first and the most important stitch to master is crocheting. A chain stitch is used in various more advanced crocheting and stitch designs. Begin by tying a slipknot. Put your crochet hook into the knot and spin it a quarter turn clockwise, pulling up the yarn with the hook. Grasp the yarn and pull it through the slip knot. That is the length of one chain stitch.

Chain color change (ch color change)- The technique of changing yarn colors when crocheting is known as chain color change (ch color change). Changing colors at the beginning of a row, if feasible, makes it easier to conceal the yarn tail while completing. Continue to work the chain stitch and pull the loop up with the new color to change colors. If you are worried about stability, tie the ends of the old and new yarn together, but make sure the knot is on the backside of your crocheting.

Cluster stitch- A cluster stitch is a collection of crochet stitches crocheted together in the same loop and then connected at the top to form a triangle. A cluster stitch resembles an upside-down shell stitch, and the two stitches are often combined in designs.

Crocodile stitch- The crocodile stitch looks like crocodile scales and adds a distinctive texture to your crocheted creations. Begin with a foundation of v-stitches to crochet a crocodile stitch. The crocodile stitch's scales are made by double crocheting numerous stitches in each of the v-stitches' posts. As you proceed, double crochet in the posts of the v-stitches and single crochet in the single crochet stitches to space out the scales.

As you proceed, double crochet in the posts of the v-stitches and single crochet in the single crochet stitches to space out the scales.

Corn stitch- A cluster stitch resembles an upside-down shell stitch, and the two stitches are often combined in designs. A corn stitch is a stitch that combines double crochets with slip stitches to create a raised bauble in the cloth.

Decrease- When a design asks for a reduction for shaping or tying off, there are a few options for getting rid of a stitch. In most cases, the pattern will tell you which kind of decrease to use since each one shapes your crocheting differently. Suppose the pattern instructs you to single crochet two stitches together or reduce one over two single crochet. In that case, you will decrease by crocheting two stitches together and passing the yarn through both stitches at the same time, allowing the second stitch to be consumed into the piece without dropping.

Double mesh- A double mesh stitch results in an open mesh fabric. Begin with a foundation chain of a two-plus-four multiple. Double crochet on the sixth stitch of the foundational row for your double mesh stitch. Chain one stitch, then skip one stitch and double crochet in the stitch immediately after the one you just double crocheted in. Carry on in this manner.

Double crochet (dc)- is a common and fundamental crochet stitch used in many more complex patterns. The double crochet stitch is approximately twice as tall as the single crochet stitch, making it ideal for looser materials. A double crochet stitch is made by drawing the yarn over the hook, putting the hook into the next stitch to be worked, and creating another yarn over, starting with a single crochet foundation row. Pull the yarn through the stitch and then yarn over. On the hook, you should then have two loops. Pull the yarn across both loops and wrap it around the hook. Finish the double crochet by pulling yarn through the final two loops on the hook.

Double love knot (dlk)- The double love knot (dlk), also known as the double Solomon's knot, produces an open, lacy weave pattern. To make this knot, extend a chain stitch on your hook to approximately 12 to 1". Reverse the yarn and draw it through the loop. In the back strand of the long loop you just created, single crochet. This pattern should be repeated.

Double Tunisian stitch (dts)- A double Tunisian stitch (dts) resembles a knitted drop stitch and provides an open, airy area in your fabric. The double Tunisian stitch is a double crochet stitch done in the first vertical bar of the preceding row's stitches.

Double treble stitch (dtr)- The double treble stitch (dtr) consists of three yarn overs before beginning the stitch and then knitting a chain stitch. Double treble stitches provide a long, open weave ideal for making scarves and afghans fast.

Drop stitch (drop st)- A drop stitch (drop st) adds texture to a design by working the stitches two rows beneath where they would usually be worked. The stitches are done normally, except for the unusual location.

Ending block (eb)- An ending block (eb) is a kind of increase or decrease stitch that uses a solid block to conclude a mesh design.

Ending mesh (em)- In filet crochet, an ending mesh closes the mesh pattern with an open mesh square.

Extended single crochet (exsc)- Extended single crochet (exsc) stitches are similar to normal single crochet stitches, but they are lengthened by wrapping yarn around the crochet hook during yarn overs.

Fasten off- Finishing your crocheted item by fastening off secures the yarn and prevents it from unraveling. Cut the yarn, leaving approximately a six-inch tail to finish. Pull the yarn through the hook's last loop. After securing the yarn with a knot, you may begin knitting in the ends and blocking your creation.

Fancy stitch- The fancy stitch, also known as lacet, is an open, v-shaped weave used in fillet crochet. Chain two stitches, then skip the following thread to crochet a fancy stitch. In the next stitch, chain two, single crochet, and skip the following stitch. After that, double crochet in the next stitch, single crochet in the next bar's gap, chain two, and double crochet in the next stitch.

Felting tips- Felting is the process that "destroys" wool yarn to produce a more substantial fabric from your crocheted wool item. When animal fibers are washed in hot water, the stitches combine to form a solid felt cloth. It has to be at least 80% wool if you want to feel anything. Crocheted items that are looser in texture tend to feel better. You may also increase the agitation of your item in the washing by passing it through with a tennis ball or an old shoe.

Filet crochet- This is a crocheted fabric that has an open mesh weave that is made out of chain stitches and double crochet stitches. In contrast to the more open mesh of the background, many fillet crochet items include a decorative design created with a solid mesh.

Four-strand braid (fsb)- this is a finishing method for crocheting projects that creates a polished, ornamental finish. A four-strand braid with an under-and-over pattern, in which strands from the outside are brought beneath the two inside strands and then over the right inner strand. Braids with four strands create strong straps or ornamental embellishments.

Fluffy stitch (fluffy st)- When working in a chain stitch, pull up the loop in the stitch below to make a fluffy stitch. This method produces a lengthy, fluffy stitch ideal for crocheting blankets or decorations because of the delicate dimension of the thread.

Foundation double crochet (fdc)- A foundation double crochet (fdc) is a stitch that provides a foundation row from which you may continue crocheting. Because of its height, the foundation double crochet creates a very strong foundation row. Begin by making a four-stitch chain. Then, in the fourth stitch, put the hook. Make a loop in the yarn and draw it up. Re-knit the loop and repeat the process. On the hook, you should now have three loops. Re-knit the yarn and pull it through one loop on the hook. Yarn over and pull the hook through two loops. To finish one foundation, double crochet stitch, yarn over, and pull through the two loops on the hook one more.

Front cross-stitch (fcr or cr st): Skip a stitch and double crochet around the preceding stitch to make a front cross-stitch. Then, in the skipped stitch, double crochet. This stitch makes an "X" design out of a sequence of stitches.

French Knot- A French knot is an embroidery stitch used to add decorations to crocheted items. Use yarn or an embroidery or yarn needle to create a French knot. Wrap the yarn around the needle three times (from back to front) after running the needle through the cloth from back to front. Run the needle back through the wraps and into the cloth at the beginning of your stitch. The French knot produces a raised stitch on the fabric's surface.

Front loops (fl)- Front loops are on top of the crochet stitch closest to you. Picking up two loops of the preceding stitch is how most crochet stitches are made. Only put the hook into the front loop of the stitch to work in the front loop, then continue with the stitch as directed by the pattern.

Front post- The vertical part of a crochet stitch is called the front post. Put your hook from the front to the rear of the item and carry it around the post to the front again to crochet around the front post. Finish with double crochet. Finish with double crochet.

Half double crochet (hdc)- To create a half double crochet stitch, first perform a yarn over and then put the hook into the next stitch to be crocheted. Re-knit the yarn and drag it through the stitch. Pull the yarn from three loops on the hook and yarn over one more. Although the half-double crochet stitch is basic, it produces a beautifully textured design.

Gauge- The gauge represents the number of stitches per inch in crochet. Personal tension, needle size, and yarn type may affect gauge. Because these three may differ from the designer's gauge while designing the pattern, it is essential to crochet a sample and test the gauge to ensure that your final product is appropriately proportioned according to the pattern.

High stitch- A high stitch is similar to other crochet stitches, but it is lengthened by adding a simple chain, resulting in a more open weave. Put your hook in the next vertical bar and yarn over to create a high stitch. Continue in this manner by pulling the yarn through, chaining one, and so on.

Joining squares- Joining squares is the technique of connecting Granny Squares to make a pattern, blanket, or another item. A whipstitch seam or a blanket seam may be used to connect squares. You may either slip stitch the seams or single crochet the edges of the squares together. There are various methods to connect squares depending on the seam required and the crocheter's abilities.

Increase- Increases are used to add a stitch to a row, allowing for the shape of a crocheted object. Working two stitches into the single stitch beneath is how you increase. When using a single crochet stitch, for example, after completing one crochet stitch, go back into the same stitch and single crochet once again. One stitch has been completed.

Knotting off- Various methods connect squares depending on the seam required and the crocheter's abilities. Knotting off is a technique for fastening off yarn at the conclusion of a project. Leave a six-inch tail on your yarn before cutting it. Pull the tail through the final stitch, done with your hook. To keep it secure, pull it tight. Weave the tail in. Fasten off is another term for fastening.

Long single crochet (long sc)- Put the hook in the next stitch and draw up a long loop to make long single crochet (long sc). Pull the yarn across both loops on the hook and yarn over. A single long crochet stitch may be used to create patterns, shape, and alter stitch lengths.

Lacet—also known as a fancy stitch. A lacet stitch produces an open, lacey weave in the form of a v in fillet crochet. Chain two stitches, then skip the next stitch to crochet a lacet. In the next stitch, single crochet, chain two and skip the following stitch. After that, double crochet in the next stitch, single crochet in the next bar's gap, chain two, and double crochet in the next stitch.

Long double crochet (long dc)- Like the long single crochet, the long double crochet may be used to change the lengths of stitches within a row, producing visual patterns in the crocheted item. Begin with a yarn over to create a lengthy double crochet stitch. Pull up a long loop on the hook by putting the hook into the next stitch. Pull the yarn through the two loops on the hook twice more.

Open fan stitch- A beautiful, complex lace design is created using an open fan stitch. For the open fan stitch, the foundation chain should be a multiple of 10 added to 6. Chain stitches, single crochets, and double crochets are repeated in a pattern to produce a textured fan design using the open fan stitch.

Love knot- A love knot stitch, also known as Solomon's Knot, produces an open lace design. Make two chain stitches after starting with a slip stitch. In the second chain from the hook, do single crochet. Pull the loop up to about 12 to 1 inch in length. Make a yarn over and pull the yarn through at the base of the stitch. Make a single crochet in the lengthy loop's middle.

Picot stitch (p)- Picot stitch (p) is created by chaining three or four stitches in single crochet and then slip sewing it into the top of the chain. A picot stitch produces an eyelet or little bauble border.

Pompoms- Pompoms are fluffy yarn balls that are used as decorations. Pompoms are created by winding yarn around three fingers in a continuous loop until the pompom is appropriate. Then, maintaining the form of the coiled yarn, slip it off your fingers. Tightly knot a piece of yarn around the center of the loop of yarn using the same color yarn. Cut the loop so that the yarn ends stretch out to form the pompom.

Place marker (pm)- In crochet designs, place marker implies that you should leave a marker, either by tying on a scrap of yarn or using a plastic place marker so that you can locate that stitch or position later. Place markers are often used to show where sleeves or seams will be added, as well as where you will take measurements. Place markers may also be used to indicate the start of rounds or other significant dates.

Popcorn stitch: This stitch makes a raised bauble on your cloth that resembles popcorn. Work three double crochets in the same area to make the popcorn stitch, drop the loop from the hook, and put the hook into the first double crochet, pulling the loop through to tighten the stitch.

Reverse popcorn stitch (rpc)- The reverse popcorn stitch (rpc) is crocheted such that the bauble is elevated on the wrong side of the item instead of the front, leaving a dip on the right side of the cloth. In the same stitch position, yarn overs and double crochets are used to make the reverse popcorn stitch. A chain stitch is used to join the additional stitches together.

Puff stitch (puff st)- A puff stitch adds texture to your crochet item by creating a raised oval. A puff stitch is made by half-closing multiple double crochet stitches in the same stitch and then connecting them to close them. You may also make a puff stitch by knitting multiple yarn overs in a single stitch before closing it.

Reverse single crochet (reverse sc)- The single reverse crochet, often known as the crab stitch, produces a rounded edge. The reverse single crochet stitch is similar to the single crochet stitch, but it is done from left to right rather than right to left.

Technique of rings and strands—also known as tatting. The rings and strands technique is a tatting lace technique that makes medallions, picots, scrolls, and other lace designs using rings and Josephine knots.

Technique of rings and chains—also known as tatting. The rings and chains technique is a tatting lace technique that uses a mix of rings and chains to produce scrolls, medallions, and other lace designs using picots, double stitches, and double chains.

Running stitch- The needle is threaded in and out of the cloth in a straight line to create a running stitch. A running stitch may be used for appliques, seams, and embroidered decorations in crochet. Simply thread the needle and run it beneath the stitch posts.

Shell Stitch- A shell stitch is a lacy stitch with a curved edge that resembles a shell. The shell stitch has many variations, each producing a slightly distinct pattern or form for the shell. Basic shell stitches are made up of a chain stitch, a pattern of two double crochet stitches, and two additional double crochet stitches all worked together in one stitch.

Satin Stitch- Satin stitch is an embroidery stitch often used to fill in open areas such as the centers of flowers in a floral design. The satin stitch is made by wrapping the thread around the center of the crocheted stitch with the threaded needle. Satin threads are stitched together closely in a circular manner to create a continuous line of embroidery around the required region.

Single crochet (sc)- Single crochet (sc) is a fundamental crochet stitch and one of the first stitches that most crocheters learn. The single crochet is made by putting the hook through into the second chain in the row after starting with a basic chain as a base row. Pull the yarn on your hook through the loop and yarn over. Re-knit the yarn and pull it through both loops on your hook. It is only one crochet stitch.

Slip stitch- A slip stitch is a simple crochet stitch that may be used for seaming two pieces together, connecting parts to create a ring or attaching Granny Squares, and adding decorations, among other things. Put your hook (with a current stitch on it) into the area where you wish to put a slip stitch to create a slip stitch. Pull your yarn through your item and the current stitch on your hook after hooking it.

Tapestry crochet- Tapestry crochet involves using several strands or colors of yarn to create colorful textiles and patterns. Tapestry crochet derives its name from the fact that the final items resemble tapestries woven on looms. Tapestry crochet is often done using single crochet stitches to keep the weave tight and emphasize the colorwork rather than the complex stitching.

Square mesh- Square mesh is also known as open mesh, is a kind of fillet crochet that creates an open square shape. Repeats of two chain stitches and a double crochet stitch, or multiples of this pattern, form the open mesh.

Tatting- Tatting is a lace-making method that uses a mix of loops and knots to create lace. Lace edging, collars, doilies, and other decorations are often tatted. Tatting is sometimes done by wrapping strong thread around needles or shuttles and directing it through complex knot patterns.

Tassels are fringed collected decorations often seen on table runners, shawls, caps, and sashes. Wrap yarn around a piece of cardboard cut to the appropriate tassel length to make a tassel. Continue wrapping until the tassel is the thickness you want. Tie the tassel top together firmly at one end, up through the top loop, using yarn. Remove the cardboard and tie a sash by wrapping the second piece of yarn from around the width of the tassel forward towards the top. Cut the lower loop of the tassel so that the threads fall freely after the top is attached.

Three-strand braid- This is the most popular kind of braid, and it may be used in crochet to create decorations or borders for your creations. Cross the left strand across the center strand to the right to make a three-strand braid. Then, to the left, cross the right strand across the center. As you cross the strands over, switch the center strand from side to side.

Treble cluster- Make one triple crochet stitch to the beginning. Repeat in the same stitch twice more, for a total of three triple crochet stitches as the foundation row or stitch. Wrap the yarn around the hook and draw the loop through the four remaining loops on the hook to close the cluster.

Triple crochet- This is also known as treble crochet. A triple or treble crochet stitch is often employed when a lengthy crochet stitch is required. Begin by yarning over your hook twice on a foundation row. The hook should be put into the next stitch. Turn the yarn around and pull it through the stitch. Pull the yarn between two of the four loops on the needle after looping it over the hook. Rep the previous step. From this stitch, you should only have one loop left.

Triple crochet- Triple crochet (sometimes known as treble crochet) is a kind of crochet that uses three strands of yarn. When a lengthy crochet stitch is required, a treble or triple crochet stitch is often employed. Begin by yarning over your hook twice on a foundation row. The hook should be put into the next stitch. Turn the yarn around and pull it through the stitch. Draw the yarn through two of the four loops on the needle after looping it over the hook. Rep the previous step. From this stitch, you should only have one loop left.

Tunisian knit stitch (tks)- To create a Tunisian knit stitch, put the hook from front to back through two vertical stitch strands, make a yarn over, and pull the yarn through the stitch. On the front half of a row, Tunisian knit stitches would be created.

Tunisian purl stitch (tps)- The Tunisian purl stitch (tps) is created by moving the yarn forward and putting the hook into the vertical bar of the following stitch. Wrap the yarn around the hook from back to front. To create the purl stitch, pull the yarn through the stitch. Tunisian purl stitches are similar to knitting purl stitches.

Tunisian lace stitch- This is a basic lace stitch. To begin, the Tunisian lace stitch requires a multiple of three plus two stitches. Every chain on your foundation row should have loops pulled up. Pull two strands of yarn through. Make two chains. Pull four times through the yarn. To finish the row, repeat the last two steps. To close the row, chain one and pull through two stitches.

Tunisian Stitch- The Tunisian simple stitch, often known as the Afghan stitch, is a basic crochet pattern that resembles small squares with a vertical bar. The Tunisian simple stitch necessitates using an afghan hook with a cap at the end to keep stitches in place.

V-stitch is a simple crochet stitch that produces a beautiful v-shaped design. V-stitches are useful for afghans and scarves because they have an open weave and a nice feel. A chain stitch, double crochet, and then another crochet in the same chain creates a v-stitch. The V-shape is created by combining tall double crochet stitches on each side of a chain stitch.

Turning Chain- A turning chain is made between rows of crochet to aid in the transition from one to the next. After turning your work, the turning chain will assist raise your yarn to the proper height for you to start working in the first stitch of the following row. As a result, the length of the turning chain will be determined by the project's gauge and the stitches utilized.

Weaving- Adding the final touches to a crochet work involves weaving in the yarn ends. Weave the tail of the yarn through the "v" created by stitches, a few stitches at a time, using a tapestry needle. Make an effort to weave the end in a hidden location on the back of your crocheting. Trim the excess yarn after weaving it through many stitches.

Yarn over hook (yoh or yo)- Yarn over refers to the process of wrapping yarn around your crochet hook. Certain stitches need more than one yarn over. Put the yarn behind the hook and then drape it over the hook through the stitch and the hook's neck to perform a yarn over. Make sure you do your yarn overs from the back to the front, not the other way around.

Woven seam- A woven seam connects two sections of crocheting that are side by side and cannot be joined with a flat seam. A woven seam is produced by sewing the yarn through matching stitches on each piece of cloth from left to right, then right to the left, using a yarn needle or tapestry and yarn. Sewing woven seams are done with the right side up and the edges of the components aligned.

Whipstitch seam- Short, basic crocheted stitches, such as single crochet, work nicely with a whipstitch seam. To make a whipstitch seam between two crocheted items, pull the yarn through the inner loops of the two parts' corresponding stitches. For the remainder of your seam, repeat in the following stitch down. The whipstitch is stitched with the parts stacked on top of each other, while the woven seat is made with the pieces flat next to each other.

Wrapping- Depending on the stitch, yarn may need to be wrapped around the hook two or more times. A double crochet stitch, for example, requires the yarn to be looped around the hook twice. Three times a triple crochet stitch. When wrapping the yarn, wrap it from back to front, much like a yarn over, to maintain your stitches moving in the same direction.

Chapter 4: Types of Crochet

Knitting may seem to be the monarch of the yarn world, but crochet has its own set of methods and finishes that knitting lacks. Crochet's beginnings are a little hazy, but we do know that it was first seen in early nineteenth-century Europe and was known as "shepherd's knitting."

Crochet was employed for utilitarian goods during WWII, such as netting and under helmet covers for troops, in the 1950s. When money and resources were limited, it was also used to decorate gowns and caps as a means for ladies to refresh their appearance. Crochet materials were popular in the 1960s, and many ladies crocheted their shift dresses and pantsuits. The granny square became more fashionable in the 1970s, with dresses, jackets, and hooded sweatshirts fashioned solely of the tiny adaptable patterns. Crochet was popular in the 1980s with thick cardigans and fete-style toys. Still, it faded in the 1990s, and now it is making a contemporary return with sophisticated homewares, wonderful children's toys, and lovely apparel for men and women.

There are many more kinds of crochet than the ones mentioned, but here are a few you may be interested in.

1. Amigurumi Crochet

This Japanese crochet art form involves creating tiny stuffed animals from crocheted or knitted yarn. Nuigurumi means stuffed doll in Japanese. Amigurumi is a kind of yarn-based doll or toy. Popular amigurumi themes include Plant vs. Zombies, Hello Kitty, and Mario Kart.

Things that you can make by using the amigurumi type of crochet

– Children's toys

– Fan items

– Larger novelty cushions and homewares

2. Aran Crochet

Cabled or ribbed crochet is thick with interlocking cables typically used to create sweaters, beanies, and scarves. Aran is also a yarn weight, so keep that in mind when you see it in a design. Aran is when you see someone wrapped beneath a large, warm blanket.

Things that you can make by using the Aran type of crochet

– Scarves

– Blankets

– Jackets

– Lapgans

– Coats

3. Bavarian Crochet

Crochet this stitch in rounds like granny squares. It makes a thick fabric with softer color transitions than granny squares. Each segment has a base row of clusters and a top row of shells.

Things that you can make by using the Bavarian type of crochet

– Shawls

– Blankets

4. Bosnian crochet

Bosnian crochet uses just the crochet slip stitch, performed in various preceding row's stitch sections. You may purchase Bosnian crochet hooks or use ordinary crochet hooks. Shepherd's knitting I.T. also resembles knitting. It is not a fashionable style right now, and it seems knitted.

Things that you can make by using the Bosnian type of crochet

– Scarves

– Smaller items because it is very time consuming

– Beanies

5. Bullion Crochet

This particular crochet stitch is made by wrapping several yarn wraps around a long hook to create a characteristic 'roll' pattern. In general, bullion crochet is used for motifs rather than cloth. It produces a thick, consistent, circular motif style.

Things that you can make by using the Bullion type of crochet

– Motifs for decoration

– Stiff items like placemats

6. Broomstick Crochet

The stitches are created around something long and broad, like a broomstick handle, and are crocheted using a conventional crochet hook. Broomstick lace is now mostly done with a thick dowel or large crochet hooks. Broomstick lace is a lovely and unusual crochet technique to master.

Things that you can make by using the Broomstick type of crochet

– Throw blankets for decoration

– Delicate shawls

7. Bruges Crochet

Bruges lace is made by crocheting 'ribbons' of lace together. In acid-proof paper-wrapped cabinets, most grandmothers have handmade Bruges crochet things.

Things that you can make by using the Bruges type of crochet

– Intricate shawls

– Tablemats

– Embellishments for clothing

8. Clothesline Crochet

Traditional crochet stitches are crocheted over a thick rope or clothesline length of thick twine to create baskets and circular mats. This is a traditional trial method from Africa and Nepal.

Things that you can make by using the Clothesline type of crochet

– Baskets

– Structural wall hangings

– Mats

9. Clones Lace Crochet

This type of crochet was developed because it was faster and simpler to make than needlepoint lace. Clones crochet includes the Clones knot. Clones lace is a useful crochet technique that was employed during wartime.

Things that you can make by using the clones lace type of crochet

– Delicate dresses and tops

– Openwork scarves

10. Cro-hook Crochet

Cro-hook crochet is done using a double ending hook. It enables the crocheter to work stitches on either end of their creation, with no right or wrong sides. This is also known as Cro-knit. This technique, like Tunisian, produces superb colored work not possible in other crochet shapes.

Things that you can make by using the Cro-hook type of crochet

– Washcloths

– Baby blankets

– Scarves

11. Filet Crochet

This is a chain and double crochet style. You fill in the blanks in a grid-like pattern to create images. The full and empty squares of the cloth may be used to incorporate pictures in a fillet crochet.

Things that you can make by using the filet type of crochet

– Cushions

– Baby blankets

– Handbags

– Jackets and kimonos

12. Finger Crochet

Finger crochet is similar to finger knitting in that it is crocheting without the hook! It is a kind of hand-woven cloth in the manner of crochet stitches. Finger crochet is enjoyable when you first start, but since the final tension is relatively loose, you will probably want to switch to a hook and create more adaptable items sooner rather than later.

Things that you can make by using the finger type of crochet

– Basic scarves

– Simple string bags

13. Freeform Crochet

This crochet technique is made without using a pattern or an established plan. Crochet in this style is highly organic and creative. Note that this approach may not be for you if you are a control freak. If you struggle without directions or a strategy, stay away from freeform.

Things that you can make by using the freeform type of crochet

– Art pieces

– One-off clothing times

14. Hairpin Crochet

This is similar to a broomstick crochet, but the crochet piece is held taut between two thin metal rods and crocheted with a conventional crochet hook. This method was named after the metal hairpins that were used when it was developed. This technique produces a unique final fabric.

Things that you can make by using the hairpin type of crochet

– Shawls

– Wraps

– Delicate scarves

15. Micro Crochet

This contemporary crochet technique is done with very fine thread and very fine crochet hooks. This is a delicate project that is perhaps best suited to more patient crocheters.

Things that you can make by using the micro type of crochet

– Teeny tiny things

– Talisman

– Embellishments

16. Overlay Crochet

A method in which stitches are added to a foundation of crochet to produce a raised design. This gives us many options for colorwork that is both beautiful and complex.

Things that you can make by using the overlay type of crochet

– Potholders

– Handbags

– Wall hangings

17. Pineapple crochet

This is more of a generic stitch and form design than a method. Pineapples may be used to create scarves, doilies, and even clothes in crochet. Once you have figured out how to identify a crochet pineapple, you will see them all over the place. This stitch technique gained popularity in the 1970s.

Things that you can make by using the pineapple type of crochet

– Wraps

– Dresses

– Shawls

– Tops

18. Stained glass crochet

Almost identical to overlay crochet, but the top portion is typically done in black yarn to give a stained glass effect. This is a distinctive and eye-catching manner.

Things that you can make by using the stained glass type of crochet

– Thick, sturdy items

– Handbags

– Winter scarves

19. Symbol crochet

This pattern is also known as chart crochet and is included in many Japanese stitch manuals. It is a precious ability to acquire since you can use any crochet symbol book in any language to complete the projects simply by following the pattern. Note: Your life will change once you understand crochet from symbol patterns.

Things that you can make by using the symbol type of crochet

– Foreign language patterns

– Difficult patterns that are hard to explain in words

– Motifs

– Intricate designs

20. Tapestry crochet

This is crochet's version of colorwork. Intarsia crochet is another name for it. There are many different ways to work in tapestry crochet, and each technique produces different results. Colorwork may be done in a variety of methods, including tapestry crochet.

Things that you can make by using the tapestry type of crochet

– Imagery based designs

– Color workpieces

21. Tunisian crochet

Tunisian crochet is comparable to knitting in that you have several active loops at any one time, and you work your loops on and off your hook, much like knitting. Tunisian crochet is done using a hook with a cord attachment or a long hook with a stopper at the end.

Things that you can make by using the Tunisian type of crochet

– Blankets

– Knit look items

– Scarves

Chapter 5: Let's Start Crocheting

5.1 Preparation

- **Beginner level**

The majority of beginner crochet projects utilize just one or two fundamental stitches. They prefer thick threads and big hooks over fine threads and tiny hooks because they are simpler to deal with. Simple shapes characterize the fabrics in this category. For crochet, a beginning project might be a basic one-color scarf with size 3 Petra or Natura Just Cotton thread.

- **Easy Level**

These designs often utilize two or more colors, and they may need finer thread and a smaller hook than beginning crafts. Easy-level crafts may be made using the same thread and hook as beginning projects, but they may contain a sequence of pretty difficult stitches. It is also possible that they will take longer to finish than beginning tasks. For example, a multi-color striped scarf made using five size threads, DMC Petra would be a suitable project for this ability level.

- **Intermediate Level**

These designs need more crochet expertise than simple crafts and utilize a range of methods and stitch patterns that are more complex. Color changes may occur more often in intermediate designs than in simple ones, but the complexity of the stitch patterns usually determines the degree of difficulty. Again, the designs may demand a variety of threads and hooks. Garments need shaping and may require buttonholes and other features that are not included in simple designs. A cardigan sweater with buttonholes, V-neck, bust shaping, three or more stitches, and a picot edging would be a suitable project for this level.

- **Experienced Level**

Non-repeating patterns and multi-color methods are used in these designs, techniques, complex stitch patterns, and dimensions. Fine threads and tiny hooks are required. Garments often have more increases and reductions in stitch counts to achieve a precise shape. In most cases, they feature intricate finishing stitches. This level's project would be a form-fitting, lacy sweater with buttonholes and inset pockets made using size 20 thread and a lace stitch pattern.

5.2 Crocheting in Rounds vs. Rows

The majority of crochet crafts are done in the round or rows. As the name implies, crocheting in rounds starts with a circle and works outwards; this method is often used to create caps, circular vests, and other round items. Crocheting in rows involves making square and rectangular things like scarves and blankets by working one row, then the next (usually turning the work, which will be described further down). Items that need shaping, like shawls, often knit in the round but with increases and reductions. An essential thing to remember right now is that it is usually better to learn how to crochet rows before moving on to rounds, which is done in this tutorial.

5.3 How to Begin Every Project

A slip knot will appear in almost every crochet creation. (Tip: There are some variations, especially when it comes to specialized crochet methods.) One such example is the magic ring, a method of starting projects in the round rather than in rows. Even if you choose that method, others begin with a slip knot. Learn this first, then go on to the next step.)

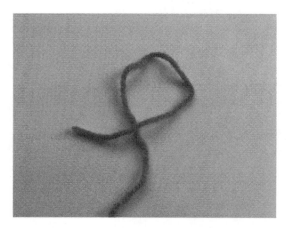

Make a loop with the loose end of the yarn, crossing it over the top of the end that is still connected to your ball of yarn.

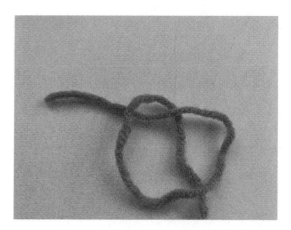

Pinch the loop's top and pull it down vertically until the portion where the yarn looped over itself is in the loop's center. You should finish up with something that resembles a pretzel.

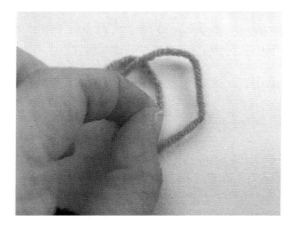

Pinch the vertically running center yarn through that "pretzel." Pull it through.

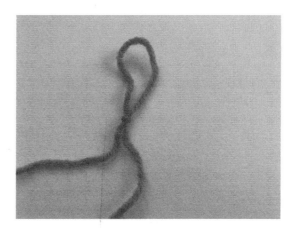

You will end up with a knot and a big loop above it after drawing that yarn through.

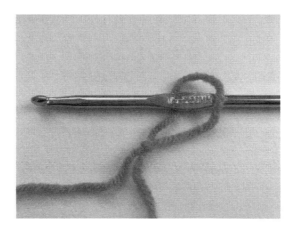

Through the loop, put your crocheting hook from right to left.

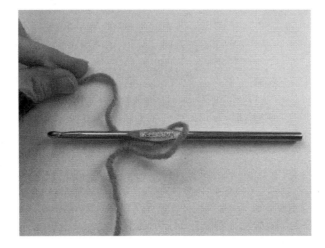

To tighten the loop, pull on the yarn's loose end.

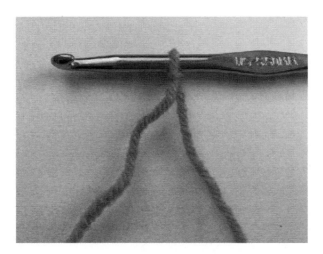

This is how you will start your crochet project now that you have made your slip knot.

How to Crochet a Chain?

Similarly, nearly every crochet item you undertake will begin with a chain. Even projects that are completed in stages may start with a short chain. Understanding how to crochet a chain is the first step toward learning how to crochet properly.

Tip: Even if you have grown used to using your crochet hook, you may discover that learning how to handle the yarn seems uncomfortable at this point. It all comes down to the amount of tension you have in both of your hands while you work. Recognize that you will get used to it. Above is an example of holding the yarn between your second and third fingers. Look at videos of other individuals handling their yarn to get a sense of their choices. Find the methods that are most effective for you. There is no correct or incorrect way to hold your crochet yarn or hook.

5.4 Yarn Over

This is a phrase you will hear a lot in crochet, so it is better to learn it immediately. The term "yarn over" refers to bringing the working yarn (the portion connected to the ball of yarn) over the top of the crochet hook and gripping it with your hook's head. "yo" is a common abbreviation for it. Here's an example of what it looks like:

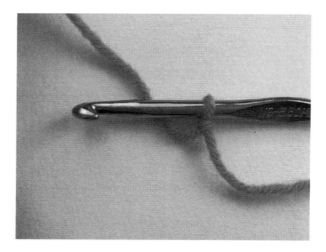

Under the bottom of the crochet hook, bring the yarn that is still connected to the ball of yarn.

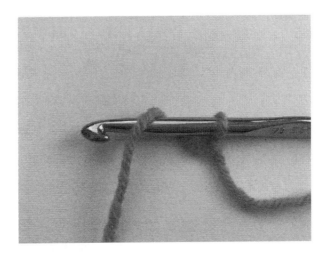

Bring the yarn over the crochet hook's top.

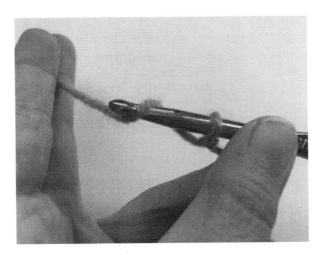

To grab it, bring it up beneath the hook's head.

5.5 Learn How to Read the Crochet Patterns

You can make crochet things using the fundamental stitches for the rest of your life and never need to read a crochet pattern. On the other hand, most individuals desire to learn to read crochet patterns at some time in their lives since it allows them to create the items they see on Pinterest and in books. As you go further into the crochet world, you will see that it has its vocabulary.

Learning this language may be intimidating at first, but it will become second nature after getting over the first learning curve. Consider this: you may not have realized that medium-weight yarn is called "worsted" and has a designated number of "4" until you started reading this text. You have it now. You already know the fundamental stitch is called "single crochet," You will soon discover it is abbreviated as "sc." You will see that abbreviation in crochet designs, and it will all make sense to you eventually.

Take your time, study the fundamentals, determine the best next steps for learning more, and go from there.

5.6 Your First Crochet Projects

After familiarizing yourself with your supplies and mastering the chain, slip knot, and at least one fundamental crochet stitch, you can create several things. Anything square or rectangular is fair game, and it is also excellent practice for learning these stitches.

All you have to do now is:

- Choose a project.

- Let's suppose you wish to knit a scarf or a washcloth.

- Crochet a chain about the same width as the item you want to create, if not a little longer.

- Choose your stitch (double crochet or single crochet, for example). Make your initial stitch in the appropriate section of the chain. Work your initial double crochet into the third chain from the hook, for example, if you are using double crochet. Then, all the way to the finish, work double crochet stitches into each chain.

- Make a twisting chain. (Make sure the length of the turning chain matches the stitch you are working with; for example, if you are working in double crochet, the turning chain should be three chains long.) Turn the job around. Across the row, double crochet into each stitch.

- Repeat the preceding step until the object reaches the desired length: square for a washcloth or extremely long for a scarf.

- Continue to practice!

Tip: Once you have completed several items using the same crochet stitch (many single crochet washcloths, numerous double crochet scarves, etc.), you may broaden your abilities by combining stitches in the same creation. For example, repeat a row of double crochet, a row of single crochet, and a row of treble crochet. Make sure the turning chain at the end of each row matches the height of the stitches you will be using in the following row (a turning chain of 3 if you are about to start a row of double crochet) and that all of the stitches are the same height within one row (double crochet in the entire row.)

Chapter 6: How to Crochet for Left-Handers

Because they learned from a right-handed crocheter, many left-handed crafters who started to crochet generations earlier had to learn the craft "backward" from their natural method. That is no longer required in today's world. There are instructors, tutorials, patterns, and more for left-handed crocheters.

6.1 Basic Understanding of Crochet for Left-Handed People

Right-handed crochet is almost identical to left-handed crochet. Left-handed crocheters use their left hand to grasp the crochet hook and their right hand to grip the yarn. It is comparable to learning how to hold the hook (in either "knife grip" or "pencil grip") and handle the yarn as a right-handed crafter; pay attention to your instructors and tutorials, but also find out what works best for you.

Almost all crochet patterns and symbol charts and most crochet tutorials are designed for right-handed crocheters. Left-handed crochet follows the same instructions as right-handed crochet, but in the other way.

This implies that row one will be put into the foundation chain from the left side and moved towards the right as you work rows. As a left-handed person, this should come naturally to you. It also implies that while you are crocheting in rounds, you will be working clockwise rather than counter-clockwise like righties.

6.2 Step-by-Step Chain

STEP 1 Start with a slip knot.

STEP 2 Yarn over. It is important to remember that as you "yarn over" in your crochet work, you will be scooping your yarn clockwise with your hook.

STEP 3 Pull the hook through the loop. Here, you will scoop the yarn in a clockwise direction.

STEP 4

Repeat the second and third steps; each repetition is one chain.

6.3 Step-by-Step Single Crochet

STEP 1 Make a foundation chain in whatever length you choose.

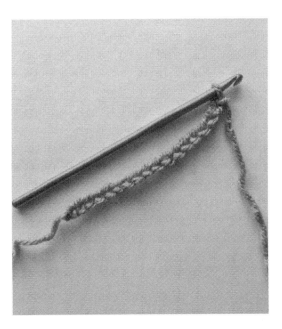

STEP 2 Hook into the second chain from the hook. You will hold your hook in your left hand with the chain extending to the right, and you will put the hook into the second chain to the right of the hook.

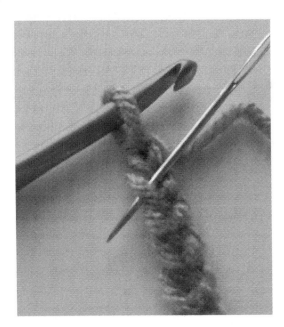

This picture shows how you will go into the chain with your hook; now, you have one strand below two stands on the top of the hook.

STEP 3 Yarn over.

STEP 4 Draw a loop across it. After this stage, your hook will have two loops.

STEP 5 Yarn over.

STEP 6

Draw the hook through both loops. This is the first single crochet.

STEP 7

Put your hook into the next chain and repeat the third and sixth steps.

STEP 8

Repeat the seventh step across the row.

6.4 Step-by-Step Double Crochet

STEP 1 Crochet a base or foundation chain of any length you choose to.

STEP 2 Yarn over.

STEP 3 Hook into the fourth chain from the hook. Working from left to right away from your hook, this is the fourth chain to the right.

STEP 4 Yarn over.

STEP 5 Draw a loop across it. You should have three loops on your hook at the end of this stage.

STEP 6 Yarn over and then draw the hook through the first two of the three loops.

STEP 7 Yarn over and then draw on the hook through the two loops. You have finished your first double crochet.

STEP 8 Rep steps 4–7 for the next stitch. Yarn over and then put the crochet hook into the next stitch.

STEP 9 Repeat the eighth step across the row.

STEP 10 Turn your work. Chain 3 for the turning chain.

STEP 11 Yarn over and then put the hook into the next stitch.

In the following picture, you can see that you are crocheting your following stitch into the 3rd chain of the preceding row's turning chain. This guarantees that the stitch count is accurate and that the form does not become triangular. Repeat the double crochet stitches all the way down the row.

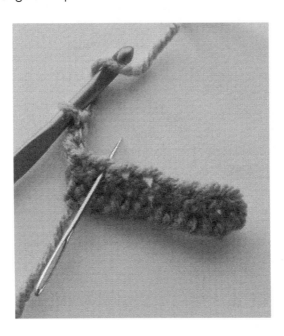

6.5 Important Tips for Left-Handed Crocheters

This image shows the "wrong side" of the double crochet stitch, further explained.

- Leave the starting yarn tail hanging at the beginning of every piece (do not crochet over it); watch for that tail as a signal when a pattern specifies the "wrong side" or "right side" of the work. When the tail is at the bottom right corner, it is on the "right side."

- Remember that you will "scoop the yarn clockwise" every time you yarn over.

- Left-handed crochet may be done using both written and graphic patterns. You may use the inverted picture to reference when working with charts and graphs.

Chapter 7: Tips and Tricks to Crocheting

7.1 How to Avoid Tangles and Improve Tension

Turn the Skeins into Small Balls of Yarn Before Start Crocheting

If you are eager to get started on your project, you may be tempted to tear the tag of your skein of the yarn and begin crocheting. You can do the crocheting with skeins of yarn, but in many instances, taking the effort to wind the skein into a ball first can provide better outcomes. This is particularly true for newcomers.

Compared to skeins, yarn balls offer a few advantages:

- Tangles should be avoided at all costs. Yarn skeins that are pulled from the center may tangle easily towards the end. Yarn balls are less prone to tangling.

- Improve the tension. If you are having trouble getting even tension, consider working with a ball of yarn instead of a skein.

You may use ball winders to assist you with this job, but you can also do it by hand.

7.2 Removing a Few Obstacles Will Make All The Difference

Remove the following obstacles before you crochet:

- Long hair: If you have long hair enough to get in the way of your crocheting, make sure it is combed and tied back before you begin. This keeps your hair from becoming knotted while you are working.

- Jewelry: Before you start crocheting, you should take off any jewelry you have on, particularly rings and bracelets. Yarn may tangle with jewelry and obstruct your progress.

- Cats: Keep cats out of the room while you are crocheting if at all feasible. A cat can't seem to stay away from a spinning ball of yarn. A cat may easily ruin a crochet creation.

7.3 Unravelling Tips

Position the Yarn Properly.

Place the ball of yarn in such a way that it can simply unravel as you crochet.

- If you are crocheting at home in a cozy recliner, you may keep the ball of yarn on your lap or at your feet, according to your preference.

- Put the ball of yarn in a tote bag if you crochet on an aircraft or in a moving car to prevent it from rolling about and unwinding.

- Do not be afraid to unravel: if you make a mistake a few rows back, pull out the stitches up until that point and start again.

7.4 Hook Precious Tips

Crocheters who are new to the craft tend to work too firmly or too loosely.

- Choose a bigger crochet hook if your work is too tight.

- Choose a shorter crochet hook if your work is too loose.

- Please remember that the hook size shown on the yarn label is just a guideline.

- Experiment with hooks before beginning a project. When creating gauge swatches, now is the best time to do so.

Avoid Changing Hooks in the Middle of a Project.

Throughout your project, you want your stitches to remain uniform. You run the risk of generating inconsistencies if you swap hooks. Even little variations in hook size from one manufacturer to the next may be troublesome.

- Manufacturers do not always use the same hook size.

- The way you form your stitches or handle the hook may be affected by minor variations in a hook shape.

You should also try Ergonomic Crochet Hooks. Ergonomic hooks for Crochet are made to be as comfortable as possible. If you can locate an ergonomic hook that you like, it may make your crocheting time more pleasant than it otherwise would be.

- Make Gauge Swatches if You Have the Time

- You may be tempted to believe that gauge swatches for crocheting are pointless. It is the most critical aspect of the project, especially if it is a garment. If you omit the gauge swatch, your work will certainly be too small.

7.5 Tricks To Creating Original And Stunning Pieces.

Do not Be Afraid to Experiment!

There are no "crochet inspectors," and nothing bad will happen to you if an experiment fails. Experimentation and practice are two of the most effective methods to get beyond the novice stage. Consider the following examples of basic experiments:

- Change the colors in a pattern.

- Try to choose different yarns.

- Details may be added or subtracted: If a design asks for fringe, use an edge instead, or add a flower to a plain hat.

Do not be scared to attempt more complicated experiments as you gain more knowledge:

- To make a basic design more interesting, add stripes.

- Use a variety of stitches.

- Customize a sweater by adding long sleeves rather than short sleeves and changing the collar.

Although some of these experiments may fail, each one will help you learn something new.

7.6 How to Improve Quickly and Have a Lot of Fun

Make Friends with Other Crocheters!

You have undoubtedly learned that there are many different ways to crochet, and they are all valid. Crocheters who have been doing it for a long time have a wealth of knowledge and experience to offer.

Find a local crochet group or look for a forum where you may learn more from these seasoned professionals. Even if you have been crocheting for a long time, there's always something new to learn.

You will make
mistakes...

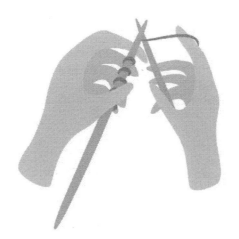

learn from them!

Chapter 8: The 10 Most Common Mistakes and Solutions

Everyone can make the same mistakes, whether they are just beginning to crochet or have years of expertise. It is quite OK to make these frequent crochet mistakes! It is important to be aware of these time sinks now to be proactive in preventing issues that may derail your initiatives.

Here are ten typical crochet errors and tips on repairing or preventing them.

8.1 Mistake #1

Crocheting in The Front Loop Only.

It is simple to make this error if you are new at crocheting. It is essential to understand where to put your hook in each stitch; it is the foundation of this art. This error may occur because you didn't completely comprehend how to crochet or because your hook slips occasionally, and you aren't experienced enough to detect the mistake straight away.

Spending additional time studying each row that you work is an excellent approach to correct this error. It may seem tiresome at first, but now that you have learned the fundamental crocheting under both loops (unless otherwise instructed), you should double-check your stitches until they are second nature.

8.2 Mistake #2

Your Work Keeps Getting Wider.

This is a common blunder that everyone makes at some point. You must remember thinking to yourself, "This is going to be very easy. It is just going to repeat the same stitch again and again!" when you first began that project. After an hour, you see that your rectangular blanket has turned into a hexagon!

This problem arises when you do not count your stitches and end up working more stitches than necessary. You may be doubling up into one stitch or a stitch crocheting in the turning chain unintentionally. The best way to avoid making this error is to count your stitches! You may either count each row as you complete it or keep a careful eye on the overall form of your work. Do not spend time working fast just to discover that you added an additional stitch ten rows back.

8.3 Mistake #3

Not Counting the Number of Rows While You are Crocheting.

Like the one before it, this point is all about not squandering your all-too-valuable time. You must count the rows the same way you must count your stitches while crocheting. I do not know about you, but

If you make the same error many times, you have effectively created and then frogged a second scarf. Using a row counter is the simplest answer to this issue. That might be a sophisticated computerized row counter that counts each row with a single click, or you could go back to basics and use a pen and notebook to create a tiny tick after each completed row.

8.4 Mistake #4

Confusing U.S. And U.K. Crochet Terms.

Crochet abbreviations conversions

With this handy table you can convert UK crochet terms to US crochet terms and viceversa

UK		US	
Chain	ch	Chain	ch
double crochet	dc	single crochet	sc
double treble	dtr	treble	tr
half treble	htr	half double	hdc
slip stitch	ss	slip stitch	ss
treble	tr	double	dc
triple treble	ttr	double treble	dtr

For example, in the United States, single crochet (sc) is known as double crochet (dc) in the United Kingdom. (Blown Mind) With this in mind, it is essential to double-check the pattern before you begin. It is recommended to contact the creator for clarification if it is not stated on the pattern. On the other hand, if you are a designer, you must clarify which words you use.

8.5 Mistake #5

Using A Different Weight Yarn and Hoping the Result to Be the Same as The Pattern.

When it comes to following a crochet design, the yarn weight is very important. If you wish to create a thick scarf from a design that calls for #6 yarn but you only have a #5, your gauge will be off, and your final item will appear different.

Each design is created with a particular yarn in mind, and even a slight weight adjustment may alter the result. It is recommended to wok your gauge swatch if you want to use up the yarn you have on hand. This will decide what changes to the pattern you need to make to be as near as feasible.

8.6 Mistake #6

Not Using the Right Hook Size.

This and the previous point are both common blunders. Using the incorrect hook size may significantly impact the result of your project. Each design is created with a particular hook size in mind, and altering it will result in stitches that are either too tight or too loose.

Make sure you read the pattern carefully to ensure you are using the appropriate size. Also, do not forget to create your gauge swatch! You may not even know you are holding the incorrect hook, but if you see your gauge swatch is inaccurate, you have just saved yourself a lot of time frogging a whole project!

8.7 Mistake #7

Not Reading Through the Whole Crochet Pattern First.

When beginning a new project, the last thing you want to do is spend time going over each line. All you have to do now is take your yarn and hook and get started! After some experience in working with crochet designs, not reading the pattern first is a mistake. However, it may not make a significant difference every time.

It is also a good idea to read the design beforehand to master a new stitch ahead of time. Although you do not have to remember each step, reading through a pattern is similar to preparing for an exam before taking it. It is always better to get right into a new crochet project!

8.8 Mistake #8

Not Knowing Where You Should Put the First Stitch or Not Counting the Starting Chain Correctly .

The beginning chain is the foundation of any crochet creation (and possibly one of the least pleasant aspects). Chaining is one of the first things you will learn to crochet, and it is also one of the most difficult.

One of the most frequent mistakes is not putting the initial stitch in the correct chain when chaining. This will result in either too many or too few stitches, and if you are not counting them (see error #2), your project will be doomed from the start. The easiest approach to prevent or solve this issue is to get extremely acquainted with chaining and counting chains.

8.9 Mistake #9

Not Working the Gauge Swatch While Following Certain Pattern or Not Making a Gauge Swatch.

The gauge swatch is an important skill to master early on. When following a pattern, this simple square may save you a lot of time and work, and it can also make your designs much simpler to follow. The gauge will determine the tension required to construct the design properly.

Make those gauge swatches (and incorporate them in your patterns), and if you discover your tension is off, spend some time correcting it by raising or reducing your hook size.

8.10 Mistake #10

Not Leaving a Long Enough Tail of Yarn.

Probably everyone's least favorite aspect of crocheting is weaving in the ends. No, you can't just snip the yarn and hope no one sees, only to struggle later because your strand is too short.

It doesn't matter whether you are tying off a project, introducing a new ball of yarn, or moving between various colors of yarn; you need to allow enough length to weave in. To make this procedure as pleasant as possible, it is recommended to leave at least 5-6 inches of yarn.

Chapter 9: Easy Crochet Patterns for Beginners

So far, you have just learned a few individual stitches. You may then learn stitch patterns, which are made up of many stitches. Because they build on the fundamental crochet stitches described above, the following are some excellent ones to start with:

9.1 Increasing and Decreasing

In crochet, the fundamental stitches may be used to decrease and increase to shape an object. A rectangular crochet shawl may be made using just basic stitches. Because you know how to create rows narrower or broader than one another, you will be able to make circular shawls, triangular shawls, half-circle shawls, and shawls in various shapes after you have learned increasing and decreasing.

9.2 Advanced Stitches

Once you have mastered increasing and decreasing, you will be well on your way to learning some of the crochet's more complex stitches. You know exactly what you will need to master cluster stitches. Bobble stitch, popcorn stitch, puff stitch, and bullion stitch are just a few textured stitches comparable to these. After learning the fundamental stitches and easy decreasing, you will be ready to study these other kinds of stitches.

9.3   How to Crochet in Round

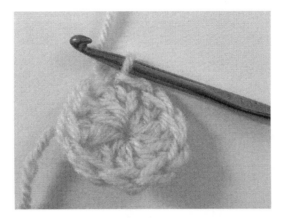

Crocheting in the round is accomplished using the same fundamental stitches you have learned so far. When working in the round, the manner a project begins is different, and you must employ strategic increasing to ensure that it grows properly. You are ready to learn how to crochet in the round if you have previously mastered some fundamental crochet stitches and how to increase. The granny square is a traditional crochet pattern done in the round, even though it is a square. A granny square lesson may be a wonderful place to start if you are new to working in the round. It is constructed with double crochet stitches.

9.4   Working in Front and Back Loop Only

When learning to crochet, it is recommended that you put your hook into "both loops" of your crochet stitch. This makes things simpler while you are first learning to crochet, but you will soon discover that you may choose to work in the front loop alone or the back loop solely of any of these stitches. Each choice produces a distinct outcome; the methods are employed to generate texture, density, ribbing, and other effects.

Tip: There is a third loop in half double crochet that you may learn about. It has a knit-like feel when you work with it. Practice working in single and double crochet with just the front and back loops, then learn about the third loop in half double crochet.

9.5   Working Around Posts

You will always work into the loops of a stitch, whether you are working in both or just one, right? Yes, except when you broaden your horizons and discover how to work around a stitch's post. Post stitches are great for giving a piece some texture. Post stitches are used in two common techniques: basketweave stitch and crochet cables. As you gain experience, you will see that you may include post stitches into a variety of basic stitches (treble crochet post stitches are as common as are double crochet post stitches). You will also discover that you may stitch around the front or rear of the post; FPDC refers to double crochet around the front of the post. As a novice, this may seem daunting, but you can be confident that complex methods like this will become much simpler to grasp if you go through the fundamental stages of learning how to double crochet.

Chapter 10: Afghan Patterns

One of the most beautiful aspects of crochet is that you can make useful and beautiful objects even if you're a complete beginner. You can create several square and rectangle designs after learning only a few basic crochet stitches. You can crochet a blanket, for example.

All of these beginner-friendly crochet blanket designs were chosen with that in mind. They're made using simple crochet stitches, do not need any shaping, and come with easy-to-follow instructions. Although several excellent beginning crochet baby blanket designs are available, they are all designed to suit adults.

10.1 HDC Squares Crochet Blanket

This crochet blanket is also made out of squares. However, rather than working in a circle, you build them in rows, which some novices prefer. Half double crochet stitches make up each row. Then you just sew them all together to make a simple checkered blanket.

10.2 Battenberg Blanket

Another simple crochet afghan design is to create a large blanket out of a large number of little crochet squares. Three circular squares make up this blanket. They're easy to make and a lot of fun. The designer has a "join as you go" technique that allows you to link the squares as you work, eliminating the need to complete all of the joinings at the end.

10.3 Linen Stitch Crochet Afghan

Do not worry if you've never heard of linen stitch; it's just a combination of chain stitches and single crochet. You can accomplish it even if you're a novice. To make a square blanket, this variation is knit in the round. It's simple to make whatever size blanket you want.

10.4 Double Crochet Striped Afghan

You can make this blanket if you know how to double crochet (called treble crochet in this pattern since it's written in U.K. crochet terminology). It's not difficult to work several dc stitches into one st and miss other stitches at times. You'll have a striped blanket when you're finished.

10.5 Modified Moss Stitch Afghan Crochet

Like the linen stitch, the moss stitch creates texture by combining two basic crochet stitches. In this instance, you combine single and double crochet into a single stitch, then skip the next stitch. You keep doing it, row after row, from row to row, and across the row. It's simple to learn, and you'll be up and running in no time. You'll finish up with a lovely crochet blanket. To prevent color changes and to weave in ends, use self-striping yarn.

10.6 Easy Bulky Crochet Afghan

Double crochet and single crochet stitches are used in this crochet blanket design. On every other row of this design, you'll work several stitches into one stitch, similar to the one above, essentially producing a row of granny stitches. It's a fantastic design that even beginners can grasp. Plus, since this simple blanket is made with a very thick yarn, it comes together fast. If you use this pattern to create your first crochet blanket, you'll be extremely pleased.

10.7 Giant Granny Square Afghan Crochet

To make a simple crochet blanket design, you only need to understand how to crochet a granny square. You can make it as big as you want it to be. Because the granny square is so tolerant of variations in yarn texture, you may use whatever yarn you choose for this project.

Chapter 11: Amigurumi Crochet Patterns

11.1 What are Amigurumi Crochet Patterns

Amigurumi is a Japanese term that roughly translates as "knitted or crocheted soft toy." In the late 1800s, the Dutch are believed to have brought knitting methods to Japan, which became famous with samurai who would use the craft to adorn and construct clothing. The kawaii movement and an NHK program called Ami helped to popularize amigurumi in the 1980s. The project was an immediate success since it required a few supplies and a little room to get started. The western obsession is newer, having taken up in the early to mid-2000s, helped by video lessons on YouTube. Amigurumi may be knitted, although it's most often linked with crochet.

Basic amigurumi projects are a wonderful place to start if you're new to crochet or have never crocheted before. They're rapid, so you can get a pattern done quickly. The ones I've gathered here are as basic as they get, making them perfect for beginners. Plus, they're adorable! What more could you ask for? Let's get started with the crocheting!

11.2 What Materials Do You Need?

To make your amigurumi creations come to life, you'll need the following materials:

- Crochet hooks are a set of hooks for crocheting. A typical set will be between 2mm and 6mm thick. Because the larger the hook, the greater the holes in your creation, you'll be working with smaller hooks for amigurumi: 2-4.

- Your yarn of choice. Yarn is available in various thicknesses and is often divided into three categories: animal-fiber-based yarns such as wool, plant-based fibers such as hemp and cotton, and synthetic fiber yarns such as acrylic.

11.3 How to Make Your First Amigurumi Stitch

- **Slipknot**: You make the first loop on your hook using a slipknot. There are many approaches to this, so if one proves tricky, try another until you discover one that works for you.

-

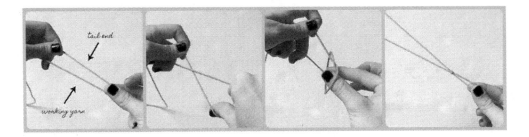

- **Making a Chain**: Many crochet projects will start with a length of chain that will serve as your foundation chain, so practice this first. Start with your hook facing up and your slip knot on top in your dominant hand. The yarn will be pulled tautly in your other hand. You'll hook the yarn, draw it through your slip knot, passing your hook in front of it, under and around it in a counter-clockwise motion. This is your initial chain, and you'll repeat the process as many times as your design requires. Counting the 'v shapes' on your chain can help you determine how many chain stitches you've created.

Tip: Make sure your stitches are even; if they're too loose or tight, you'll have problems later. To begin, you may alter the size of your hook to a bigger or smaller size to assist you.

- **Single Crochet:** (On UK designs, this is also known as Double Crochet): This stitch is ideal for amigurumi since it produces a thick fabric with no gaps, and you'll find yourself using it again and again.

- **Magic Circle:** Most amigurumi designs begin with the creation of a magic circle,' which is just an adjustable circle (typically the top of the head) where you can pull in the hole in the center rather than crocheting a circle that will leave a hole in the center that you can't modify. It takes some effort to perfect this method, but you'll be surprised at how helpful it is once you do.

magic ring   big hole

11.4 Tips and Tricks for Making Amigurumi

Amigurumi is a fantastic method for crafters to make items that others can treasure. The increase in the popularity of amigurumi may also be attributed to the availability of online media shopping channels. Not only can we share our work with other craft enthusiasts all around the globe, but it also gives individuals like myself who have never dreamed of running a small company the chance to do so.

Do not give up if you're having trouble at first. It's surprising how quickly you get accustomed to the feel and action, and it'll be second nature to you before you know it - it's a great way to spend a night with Netflix!

- Use as many patterns as possible from various designers. Each designer has something unique to give, whether tiny hints for getting the perfect amigurumi finish or various methods to create a form, all of which will help you gain experience and refine your abilities.

- It's worthwhile to devote time to taking excellent photos of your work. You've put in so much time and effort to make your lovely amigurumi; now is the moment to get the perfect picture to display your work.

11.5 What Else Can You Do with Amigurumi Techniques?

One of the greatest things about crochet is that you can create a wide variety of items after you've mastered the techniques without learning any more stitches. Aside from amigurumi, coasters, facemasks, bookmarks, baby blankets, and many other things may be made using the same methods and are simpler to create while practicing.

As you make your own home and reusable goods, as well as presents for others, many of these things may help you live an eco-friendlier lifestyle. Search for the recycled yarn if you want to be even more environmentally conscious. You can even recover yarn from old sweaters by unraveling it, soaking it, and allowing it to dry. You may also experiment with dyeing the yarn to make it ideal for your projects!

Conclusion

Crochet is an ancient skill going back to centuries named after the French term crochet, meaning "hook." Crochet is a peaceful and enjoyable activity that is simple to pick up.

You may make stunning home décor projects and fashionable items with this cool and very popular needlecraft, including tops, shawls, hats, scarves, tablecloths, doilies, and bedspreads, as well as charming baby products.

Crochet is a recognized stress reliever and one of the finest hobbies for relaxing. Sit down with some hooks and yarn when your personal life becomes a bit too much to manage.

Get lost in the stitches and enjoy the joy of seeing a creation take shape. One stitch at a time, your troubles will go away. With all its benefits, crocheting is going to give you a fun time while you watch Netflix or go for a long ride, and you will end up with a beautiful piece of your artwork.

I'm so glad you're starting your crochet journey! I actually learned how to crochet from my grandmother when I was younger. I remember sitting next to her as she worked on her projects, patiently teaching me the craft's basics.

Starting out, it can be daunting to try and learn all the different stitches and techniques, but it's also inspiring to see what you can create with just a hook and some yarn. As I got more comfortable with crochet, keeping track of my progress in a journal helped me stay motivated and see how far I had come.

That's why I created a tool that I still use - my Crochet Journal. It's been a huge help to me in my crochet journey, and I thought you might find it helpful too. The journal allows you to keep track of all the details of your crochet projects, from the simple to the more complex ones.

One of the best things about the journal is that you can record everything you need to know to recreate the project in the future. This is really helpful when you want to make something again or even modify the pattern. You can also include a picture of the completed project and a sample of the used yarn.

If you're interested in downloading a **FREE printable copy of my Crochet Journal**, scan the code at the beginning of this book and follow the instructions. I hope it helps you as much as it's helped me and that you feel your grandmother's presence as you explore this beautiful craft.

Sarah Tunisian